Flicker

P.J. Reed

also by P.J. Reed

poetry

FLICKER

COFFEE SHOP LIFE

HAIKU NATION

HAIKU ICE

HAIKU YELLOW

HAIKU SUMMER

HAIKU GOLD

Flicker

a collection of sizzling senryu by P.J. REED

Lost Tower Publications

P.J. Reed

First published in 2017

third edition 2021

by Lost Tower Publications.

P.J. Reed asserts her copyright over this collection of her work.

P.J. Reed is hereby identified as the author of this work in accordance with Section 77 of the Copyright, Designs, and Patents Act 1988.

This book is sold subject to the condition that it shall not, by way of trade or otherwise, be lent, hired out or otherwise circulated without the publisher's prior consent in any form or cover than that in which it is published.

ISBN: 9781542562201

Flicker

P.J. Reed
Writer of Warlocks. Destroyer of Worlds.

Reed is an award-winning, multi-genre author with books ranging from high fantasy, horror, to haiku. She writes the *Richard Radcliffe Paranormal Investigations* series and the *Bad Decisions* series. Reed is also the editor and chief paranormal investigator for the *Exmoor Noir* newsletter.

She holds a BAEd from Canterbury Christ Church University, an MA from Bradford University and has dabbled in psychology with the OU.

Her writing has appeared in a wide variety of online and print magazines, anthologies, and collections.

In 2015, she was shortlisted for the National Poetry Anthology award. In 2018, P.J. won the Forward Press Poetry 'Circle of Life' competition for her poem 'The Empty Chair.'

In her poetry, Reed writes of the beauty and ethereal nature of the changing countryside in her series of haiku inspired collections, photographs, and poetry.

Reed lives in Devon, England with her two daughters, two rescue dogs, and one feral cat called Sammy.

For more information about Reed please visit one of the following websites:

Horror/ Paranormal - https://pjreedwriting.wixsite.com/horror
Poetry - https://pjreedwriting.wixsite.com/poetry
Fantasy - https://pjreedwriting.wixsite.com/fantasy
Twitter - https://twitter.com/PJReed_author
Facebook - https://www.facebook.com/p.j.reedauthor

Flicker

P.J. Reed

Introduction

Senryu is an ancient Japanese poetry form, whose origins date back to the Edo period. It is a mirror on the human condition describing people and their actions in succinct, minimalist detail. Flicker is a combination of haiku and senryu, combined and updated for the modern audience. In this collection, P.J. Reed has brought together a series of poetic postcards entwining the everchanging nature of the Devon countryside with the lives of the people she has met in her travels throughout the county.

P.J. Reed has sought out the people of Devon, exploring their actions and emotions and captured a snapshot of their life in verse. Thus, creating a fascinating representation of humanity and nature.

P.J. Reed writes in traditional Japanese haiku and senryu. Each poem has three sections, where the first and last lines contain five moras, while the middle line has seven. The mora is a unit of sound in the Japanese language.

Unfortunately, due to the dissimilarities of Japanese and English language the formal writing of haiku and senryu has had to be adapted. Moras cannot be translated into English and therefore syllables are used in their place. Syllables are the nearest equivalent to moras, in Western language. Consequently, formal westernised haiku is written as seventeen syllables divided into three lines of five, seven, and five syllables.

Another difference between Japanese and westernised haiku is in the physical line structure of the poem. Haiku can be written in one or three vertical lines in Japanese, whereas in English the poem is divided into three horizontal lines.

Apart from the obvious differences in written structure, the actual essence of haiku and senryu has remained the same bridging both cultures.

Flicker

Traditional haiku does not rhyme or contain punctuation and has a juxtaposition, or cutting word, on the first or third line dividing the poem into contrasting parts. Haiku is usually written with natural and seasonal references with feelings and thoughts succinctly captured in one breath. Senryu developed from haiku.

Haiku was seen as a poetry form for the elite. While senryu was viewed as verse for the masses and became especially popular among the working people from the eighteenth century onwards. It was named after Karai Hachiemon who wrote senryu under the pen name Senryū or River Willow.

Senryu has a similar physical construction to haiku but where haiku dwells on aspects of nature and always contains a kigo or season word, senryu is a written commentary on man and the manmade. It can be comic, cynical or darkly humorous, a comment on human predicaments or human emotions.

One example of the comic nature of senryu, can be found in Karai Senryu final verse which stated -

> write me down as one who loved
> senryu,
> and loose women

In *Flicker*, P.J. Reed has taken the comic origins of senryu and reintroduced them into a modern setting, for example,

> frowning sky smiled
> people burst from houses tails
> wagging in the sun

> red faced walruses
> big-bellied and well-basted
> cooking in the sun

She has also expanded them into darker places, with commentaries of loneliness and destitution –

> alone sea watching
> white wave sweeps in and leaves a
> shining pebble gift

> the cold homeless man
> cries buy a big issue please
> dog lies on warm coat

Finally, Reed has used this book as an intriguing commentary of current affairs as seen through the eyes of the people who are living through such times.

This book is a captivating ride through the very essence of humanity.

A fantastic read.

Karen Jones

Flicker

P.J. Reed

Contents

Senryu Number	First Line	Page Number
	Biography	
	Introduction	
	The Characters	
1	a child in the park	18
2	an angry binman	19
3	an angry poet	20
4	an earringed couple	21
5	businessman panics	22
6	busy businessman	23
7	corrupted self	24
8	Costa shop writer	25
9	couples sip lattes	26
10	cross-legged he reads	27
11	crunching through gold leaves	28
12	drinking tea unpaired	29
13	eat out to help out	30
14	elderly couples	31
15	flesh-coloured facemask	32
16	fractions of Costa	33
17	grabbing toilet rolls	34
18	handsome barista	35
19	hanging from the ear	36
20	he dreams of monsters	37
21	human exhibits	38

	Flicker	
22	hungry young father	39
23	JC smiles and shakes	40
24	love on the sidewalk	41
25	melting midday sun	42
26	next door neighbour knocks	43
27	old man walks home with	44
28	on husband watching	45
29	over crowded gaps	46
30	paired and preened they fly	47
31	pandemic faux pas	48
32	queuing by the bank	49
33	red-faced walruses	50
34	reports of dying	51
35	rotund man wobbles	52
36	she is a flat white	53
37	she orders coffee	54
38	snatched quiet moments	55
39	the cold homeless man	56
40	the writer's heartbreak	57
41	tired businessman	58
42	travelling through time	59
43	two grey-haired women	60
44	unusual sounds	61
	Senryu Memories	
45	a summer puddle	64
46	alone sea watching	65
47	an absence of touch	66
48	battered walking boots	67
49	collared dove couple	68

50	dragonfly flutters	69
51	drowning with sorrow	70
52	empty mountain winds	71
53	freed to fly alone	72
54	from darkness hidden	73
55	frowning sky smiled	74
56	frowning thoughts circle	75
57	glowing orange balls	76
58	grassbound we wander	77
59	grey coloured glasses	78
60	hair whitens skin pales	79
61	half-blown wishes fly	80
62	happiness is lost	81
63	hiding in the blue	82
64	home has soft brown eyes	83
65	hungry white-tailed dove	84
66	I am loneliness	85
67	I checked my Twitter	86
68	I walk in autumn	87
69	I walk in wonder	88
70	I walk on cloud tops	89
71	in footsteps of one	90
72	internet unplugged	91
73	invisible me	92
74	labour saving life	93
75	little ginger dog	94
76	memories of you	95
77	my little cloud weeps	96
78	nighttime once more	97

Flicker

79	one thousand letters	98
80	one touch of yellow	99
81	pawprint memories	100
82	pixelated touch	101
83	plastic chair jumbles	102
84	refilling a heart	103
85	sadness comes like waves	104
86	seconds tick slowly	105
87	snatched quiet moments	106
88	softly cooing songs	107
89	steel pylons straddle	108
90	sun falls from the sky	109
91	the day is cooling	110
92	the disappointment	111
93	the night is growling	112
94	the sadness of age	113
95	the sky is falling	114
96	the yellow moon peers	115
97	touch button friendships	116
98	twenty-twenty life	117
99	umbrellas flying	118
100	winter clouds gather	119
101	wintry rain tumbles	120
102	your messages left	121
	The History of Haiku	123-4
	Glossary of Terms	125-6
	Bibliography	127
	An Interview with P.J. Reed	128-131

P.J. Reed

Flicker

Characters

P.J. Reed

        a child in the park
    runs to greet her long lost friend
       stops six feet apart

Flicker

        an angry binman
    discussing second lockdown
       a load of bullocks

Many people did not believe in the Covid pandemic. This snippet of sparkling conservation was overheard in the High Street.

an angry poet
his sonnet ends with orange
a rhyming fail

Flicker

        an earringed couple
       lean over lattes in love
         alone in the crowd

P.J. Reed

> businessman panics
> face masked and suffocating
> while his wife walks on

Some people were unable to wear the compulsory facemasks due to health reasons. Others with no health problems seemed unable to breathe in them regardless.

Flicker

busy businessman
writes his wife a postcard while
sextexting his friend

> corrupted self
> implanted and unaged
> women plasticised

Sometimes plastic surgery creates only plastic faces. Growing old naturally is a form of beauty.

Flicker

> Costa shop writer
> watches from her coffee cup
> mocha flavoured life

For my fellow Costa shop writers.

P.J. Reed

></p>
couples sip lattes
stare lovingly into phones
and forget to talk

Flicker

        cross-legged he reads
       sitting by the corner shop
        turns tattered pages

Written for the homeless man who sits reading on Exeter High Street, outside the corner shop, surrounded by donations of drink and food, mainly from kind students.

P.J. Reed

>crunching through gold leaves
>discussing toilet closures
>two angry women

Another major pandemic issue in my village was the closure of several public toilets.

Flicker

    drinking tea unpaired
    old woman sits alone as
    people hurry past

P.J. Reed

> 'eat out to help out'
> support your local café
> corona-to-go

The 'Eat Out to Help Out' Scheme was a government incentive to encourage customers to eat in restaurants or other eating establishments by giving them a discount which the restaurant then claimed back from the government. Critics said it led to a rise in Covid cases.

Flicker

        elderly couples
    sipping tea in symmetry
       love is reflected

P.J. Reed

> flesh-coloured facemask
> the shop assistant's mistake
> a horror feature

Some people made unfortunate decisions regarding their choices of facemasks.

Flicker

        fractions of Costa
   young man tells his life story
       handing pots of tea

P.J. Reed

> grabbing toilet rolls
> he weaves through the empty shelves
> clutching precious haul

One of the fascinating things about the Covid pandemic was the hoarding of toilet rolls. Society may have been collapsing but bathroom etiquette had to be maintained.

Flicker

>handsome barista
>hands out her daily latte
>which she does not like

P.J. Reed

        hanging from an ear
he his facemask swings in the wind
        protecting his chin

Some people never quite understood the concept of wearing a mask during the pandemic.

Flicker

        he dreams of monsters
     stories float on empty pages
         as his wife talks on

P.J. Reed

> human exhibits
> hidden under glass and brick
> nature has been freed

Nature revived during the March lockdown. Wild animals were seen roaming the empty streets.

Flicker

        hungry young father
    hunts melted cheese toastie prey
         wife stands forgotten

P.J. Reed

> JC smiles and shakes
> recalls times of gangland war
> and bursting cellars

JC was a poet and writer who used to 'help out' a rival gang to the Krays in his younger days. He had the scars to prove it.

Flicker

      love on the sidewalk
    alone they sit together
     man and dog unhomed

P.J. Reed

        melting midday sun
     faces bob in swimming pools
        human hippo's pod

Written while tourist watching in Crete.

Flicker

next door neighbour knocks
wants sugar with benefits
deflated souffle

P.J. Reed

> old man walks home with
> plastic bag full of food tins
> rests and rubs sore hands

At the beginning of the first lockdown, there was panic buying, and the most vulnerable suffered.

Flicker

> on husband watching
> jealous wife sweeps to his side
> brushes girl away

P.J. Reed

>over crowded gaps
>she waves from across the room
>I forget her name

An unfortunate, regular occurrence.

Flicker

        paired and preened they fly
        worshiping an orange ball
          return to sender

The tourist season brings flights of exotic creatures to Devon.

pandemic faux pas
a leopard print facemask
knickers on her nose

More fascinating choices of facemasks.

Flicker

        queuing by the bank
     covid safe and masked in black
          hostile withdrawal

P.J. Reed

>red-faced walruses
>big-bellied and well-basted
>cooking in the sun

Written in Rhodes watching a group of tourists sunning themselves by the pool.

Flicker

>reports of dying
>the new Wuhan takeaway
>a global franchise

The first reports of illness came from China. No one realised the impact SARS-Coronavirus was going to have across the world.

P.J. Reed

> rotund man wobbles
> after disappointed wife
> carrying a spoon

As witnessed in Costa.

Flicker

        she is a flat white
        he a double expresso
        a coffee conflict

she orders coffee
a fresh dark full-bodied blend
her liquid lover

Flicker

        snatched quite moments
        silence in crowded cafes
           tea mediations

P.J. Reed

> the cold homeless man
> cries buy a big issue please
> dog lies on warm coat

Flicker

        the writer's heartbreak
     his half-thought story started
          I have seen the film

P.J. Reed

> tired businessman
> takes ageing wife to dinner
> hungry for a change

Flicker

       travelling through time
       he stops to deliver news
       tells of snow next month

There is a time traveller in Crediton, Devon. He came into the café where I was writing and gave me magazines from a fortnight in the future. Then he ran off to meet the future once more.

two grey-haired women
gossip of bad hips and coughs
and sip smooth lattes

Flicker

        unusual sounds
   screams and goggles fill the park
      children have returned

P.J. Reed

Flicker

Senryu Memories

P.J. Reed

        a summer puddle
showed me my altered image
    then she looked away

Flicker

        alone sea watching
   white wave sweeps in and leaves a
         shining pebble gift

Written while visiting the beautiful Croyde beach with my eldest daughter, Sapphire. We were walking along the beachfront and suddenly and wave swooped in and when it retreated, it left one shining pebble behind.

P.J. Reed

> an absence of touch
> walking with your hand in mine
> happiness now lost

The two-metre rule was introduced in March 2020, to avoid the spread of Covid19 from person-to-person contact.

Flicker

       battered walking boots
   creak and groan with every step
        still they do not fit

P.J. Reed

        collared dove couple
     sleep on telegraph perches
          urban life stories

Flicker

        dragonfly flutters
    wings of finest cobweb silk
       seen we walk away

drowning with sorrow
my tears would fill an ocean
body why so frail

Flicker

    empty mountain winds
scatter thoughts of solitude
   still the raven calls

P.J. Reed

>freed to fly alone
>fragments of family life
>flicker through my thoughts

Life consists of flickering memories.

Flicker

>from darkness hidden
the shy moon appears and smiles
my soul companion

P.J. Reed

      frowning sky smiled
  people burst from houses tails
     wagging in the sun

Flicker

        frowning thoughts circle
     watch decisions best unmade
       chase the empty clouds

P.J. Reed

> glowing orange balls
> antennas fixed on the sky
> a pumpkin landing

I find pumpkin patches fascinating and slightly alien.

Flicker

>   grassbound we wander
>   through dreams of thundering waves
>   the land gull and I

P.J. Reed

>grey-coloured glasses
>revisiting past sadness
>ripping scars apart

Sometimes it is just wiser to forget the past and just move forward with your life.

Flicker

    hair whitens skin pales
    as I slowly fade away
    ancient oak regreens

P.J. Reed

>half-blown wishes fly
>fill the air with magic dust
>sprinkled by the wind

Flicker

    happiness is lost
taken by a falling darkness
   senryu is written

P.J. Reed

>hiding in the blue
> the watching moon surprised me
> not alone today

Flicker

        home has soft brown eyes
        and a wagging ginger tail
        we walk on unroofed

For Rupert, my beautiful, clingy, rescue dog.

P.J. Reed

      hungry white-tailed dove
watches me and shares my lunch
        people scurry by

Flicker

                I am loneliness
       the kind moon watches and sends
                a shadow friend

P.J. Reed

> I checked my Twitter
> no retweets or friend requests
> do I still exist

The blessing and curse of social media.

Flicker

        I walk in autumn
    watched by a friendly robin
      we share the morning

P.J. Reed

        I walk in wonder
watch as nature grows and breathes
     man made redundant

Flicker

        I walk on cloud tops
floating through the misted fields
     the wind calls my name

P.J. Reed

      in footsteps of one
noise of a hanging silence
      fills the emptiness

Flicker

        internet unplugged
    my house rests in the silence
         humming happily

invisible me
voices floating through the air
am I here at all

Flicker

>labour saving life
>people run on hamster wheels
>to spend labour saved

P.J. Reed

> little ginger dog
> smiles and snores his happy dreams
> duvet occupied

In memory of Fizz, my beautiful, duvet-hogging, rescue dog.

Flicker

        memories of you
    carved forever in cold stone
      etched onto my heart

P.J. Reed

> my little cloud weeps
> raindrops for my eulogy
> too soon cries the wind

Flicker

    nighttime once more and
   lonely moon asks for a friend
      my bed lies empty

P.J. Reed

        one thousand letters
   sprawled across a naked sheet
     once you wrote to me

Flicker

    one touch of yellow
    the birch leaves crumble and fall
    I walk on crunches

pawprint memories
tail wagers and ball chasers
etched into wet sand

Flicker

pixelated touch
faces float across the screen
promises of love

plastic chair jumbles
sit scattered in empty rooms
echoes of laughter

Flicker

        refilling a heart
the wintery touch of sadness
    melts in your embrace

P.J. Reed

        regrets of summer
we could have loved forever
     but you never tried

Flicker

>sadness comes like waves
>rolling on the beach
>relentless and unstoppable

P.J. Reed

        seconds tick slowly
    pale moon falls from the sky
       as the darkness fades

Flicker

        softly cooing songs
     gentle pairs of preening doves
          I am but a one

The beauty and tenderness of pairs of doves. I have a lovely breeding colony in my back garden and, sometimes, the lawn looks like I am growing doves.

P.J. Reed

        steel pylons straddle
green fields of sheep and pheasant
          aliens in grey

Flicker

        sun falls from the sky
     lost seconds hang in the air
          waiting for your smile

P.J. Reed

      the day is cooling
evening wind coos and twitters
   through our open door

Flicker

      the disappointment
    opening the chocolate tin
       and finding toffee

P.J. Reed

      the night is growling
    roars through my window
     even the moon hides

Flicker

>   the sadness of age
>   falling memories tumble
>   stolen by the wind

For the unseen casualties of Covid-19.

P.J. Reed

        the sky is falling
but darkness leaves no footsteps
       silence in stillness

Flicker

       the yellow moon peers
    from behind the dark blue sky
         awake too early

P.J. Reed

                touch button friendships
              flickering across the screen
                    contact deleted

Flicker

        twenty-twenty left
    under bursting viral cloud
       new year new covid

P.J. Reed

        umbrellas flying
playful breeze blows and snatches
   windblown shoppers squeal

Flicker

> winter clouds gather
> whispered plots on wild winds
> I would catch the sun

P.J. Reed

wintry rain tumbles
chimes against the sleeping stones
my footprints taken

Flicker

        your messages left
    hanging on a distant cloud
        minimalist love

P.J. Reed

There is always poetry and love.

Flicker

The History of Haiku

Haiku is an ancient Japanese artform dating which originated from the Heian period of Japanese culture (700-1100). In this period, it was a requirement of polite society to be able to recognize, recite, and participate in *renga* or collaborative, long poetry writing activities at social events and lavish house parties. *Renga* was one of the most important literary arts in pre-modern Japan. The verses used sound unit counts of five-seven-five and seven-seven and finished with two lines of seven sound units each. At this time, poets considered the use of *utakotoba* as the essence of creating a perfect *waka* and use of any other words were considered unbecoming of true poetry.

A *hokku* was the opening stanza of *renga*. It had a special status in the poem and was written by the host or a guest of honour. A *hokku* was composed of seventeen moras or sound units broken into phrases of five, seven and five sound units respectively. Alone among the verses of a poem, the hokku included a *kireji* or cutting-word which appears at the end of one of its three phrases. Like all Japanese writing it was written vertically down the page and not horizontally as in western writing.

In the sixteenth century, with ongoing military conflicts within Japan and the eventual rise of the Tokugawa shogunate, Japanese poetry underwent a mini revolution becoming freer and less complicated.

By the time of the great *haiku* master Matsuo Bashō (1644–1694), the *hokku* had begun to appear as an independent poem and was also incorporated in *haibun* (a combination of prose and *hokku*), and *haiga* (combining a picture with a *hokku*). In the late 19th century, Masaoka Shiki (1867–1902) renamed the individual *hokku* poem *haiku*.

P.J. Reed

A traditional *haiku* poem has three lines, where the first and last lines contain five moras, while the middle line has seven. The *mora* is a unit of sound in the Japanese language, which is the Japanese equivalent to a syllable, but it is not the same. *Moras* cannot be translated into English and therefore syllables are used in their place. When westernized, *haiku* is written as seventeen syllables divided into three lines of five, seven, and five syllables.

Traditional *haiku* does not have a title, rhyme or contain punctuation but they have a juxtaposition on the first or third line dividing the poem into contrasting parts. The *haiku* is usually written with natural and seasonal references with feelings and thoughts succinctly captured in one breath.

Glossary of Terms

Haibun	A combination of prose and haiku.
Haiga	A picture combined with haiku.
Haijin	The writer of haiku.
Haiku	Haiku is a highly structured form of Japanese poetry. In western culture haiku is easily recognisable from micro-poetry by its structure. Haiku is made of three lines. The first line contains five syllables, the second seven syllables and the third five syllables. Traditional haiku must contain certain elements such as a *kigo* and a seasonal element. It consists of a moment in nature captured and recorded.
Haiku Moment	The intense focus on one moment in time. To capture and freeze that image in haiku before it is lost or altered by the passage of time.
Hokku	The original form of haiku. The opening stanza to a *renga*. A long poem written by many people as a form of entertainment for the ruling elite of Japanese society.
Juxtaposition	When sentences are placed together with a contrasting effect.
Kigo	A word that implies the season of the haiku.
Kireji	A cutting word that denotes a break between the two parts of the haiku when writing in one-line Japanese poetry. There is no English equivalent to this although some

	poets may put a dash in their haiku to denote the change.
Koan	A *koan* is a Zen Buddhist contemplative phrase which contains a logical contradiction or paradox, designed to challenge the reader.
Mora	The *mora* is a unit of sound in the Japanese language, which is like a syllable, but not the same.
Sabi	The innate loneliness of life.
Senryu	A form of human haiku, expressing emotions or human actions. It has the same structure as haiku but does not have to contain a cutting word.
Syllable	A syllable is a single, sound unit of a word.
Tanka	A *tanka* is similar to haiku but consists of five lines and thirty-one syllables. Each line has a set number of syllables see below Line one – five syllables Line two – seven syllables Line three – five syllables Line four – seven syllables Line five – seven syllables
Utakotoba	Words suitable to be used in songs or poetry.
Wabi	The austere and severe beauty of nature expressed through writings of spiritual solitude.
Waka	Traditional Japanese poetry.

Bibliography

"The Serious Side of Senryu," Edited by Alan Pizzarelli, Simply Haiku: A Quarterly Journal of Japanese Short Form Poetry. Autumn 2006, vol 4 no 3

"Senryu | Japanese Poem," Encyclopaedia Britannica. N.p., 2016. Web. 27 Dec. 2016.

"Senryu: Refreshing The Human Spirit". Haiku North America. N.p., 2016. Web. 27 Dec. 2016.

"Simply Haiku: Quarterly Journal of Japanese Short Form Poetry – Showcase," Simplyhaiku.com. N.p., 2016. Web. 27 Dec. 2016.

"Some Senryu About Go," Kiseido.com. N.p., 2016. Web. 27 Dec. 2016.

An Interview with P.J. Reed

Do you remember writing your first words of poetry?
My writing journey has been quite an interesting one. At school, the teachers could not understand why my writing was so slow, disordered, and generally just a little off. So, I kept my creative writing very private, creating my own stories on folded pieces of paper.

My writing career really began at university, by that stage I had learnt the skills to cope with creative writing and I was finally diagnosed with global dyslexia. However, my writing confidence massively increased when doing a poetry course and being told by the lecturer that I should take up a career in poetry. This was the first time anyone had encouraged me to do creative writing and it changed the course of my life.

My first poems were heavily influenced by my reading of the romantic poets as I had yet to find my own writing style. Some were still jumbled by dyslexia but the more I wrote the more coping skills I developed and after a few years I began to focus on writing short, narrative poetry.

My journey into haiku, which is probably the type of poetry I am best known for, started quite by chance over a decade ago. I was reading the poems in a LinkedIn group and I read this intriguing short form of poetry about nature. It was succinct and beautiful, like a picture painted with words. I embarked on a haiku odyssey learning about its origins in sixteenth century Japan, the distinct rules for writing authentic haiku, and reading the works of its greatest masters such as Basho. Finally, the teaching of haiku has come full circle and I give talks on the writing of haiku.

Flicker

Does your background influence your writing?
I grew up in Bromley, Kent and had little knowledge of poetry. As I child I had a rhyming poetry book which I memorised. It was only after I moved to Devon and met previously unknown relatives that I realised writing poetry was part of my family history. One of my coal mining relatives used to write poetry in the 1950's in the back of an old blue school exercise book. It was lovely to discover that link. This move to Devon and my rediscovered heritage had a profound impact on my poetry. Much of the poetry I now write is based on experiences and observations of Devon nature.

What subjects inspire you to write?
The Devon countryside inspires much of my haiku poetry. However, my senryu is inspired by poetry by the people I see in their natural settings such as talking in cafes or on holiday. Whereas my haiku and senryu writing come from observations, the dark side of my poetry comes from an active imagination and the idea of 'What would happen if...?'

My writing process is quite simple. I write what comes into my thoughts. I think poetry should be a natural flow of words, so initially my poems are written on my phone, on receipts or anything I can access at a moment's notice when the inspiration arrives. Then later I try to decipher what I wrote as I copy them down into my 'official' poetry notebook.

Do you remember your first ever published work?
My first published poem was a long time ago. It was to be honest a terrible poem about lost love published in a collection of love poems by one of those publishers who accept every poem sent to them providing you buy the anthology. However, at the time I thought it was amazing and I could not believe my poem was

actually in a book, it was so exciting. I bought two copies and still have them in my bookcase, to remind me of my poetry journey.

What publication are you most proud to have your work published in, why?

The poetry collection I am most proud of is my haiku seasons collection exploring the changes the Devon countryside undergoes with the change of each season. *Haiku Yellow* for spring, the upcoming *Haiku Sun*, *Haiku Gold* for autumn, and *Haiku Ice,* my winter collection. It has taken me five years to finish the collection and I consider it to be my poetic symphony. The Haiku collection has spread the word of haiku to many different countries and been accepted into haiku collections which is a huge honour and something I never expected.

Do you have a favourite genre of poetry?
My favourite genre of poetry is haiku, of course! However, I love the Romantic Poets and anything that makes me laugh or think or appreciate a beautiful descriptive narrative. The poems that have been significant to me are:
'She Walks in Beauty' by Lord Byron
'If' by Rudyard Kipling
'Stop all the clocks, cut off the telephone' by W. H. Auden
'Sea Fever' by John Masefield

Do you have a favourite writing space?
My favourite writing spaces are either my desk or in the quiet corner of a noisy café.

What projects are you working on and why?
My plans as a writer are huge!

Flicker

This year the final book in my haiku seasons collection, 'Haiku Sun' is going to be published. I am working on my high fantasy novel, 'Resurgence' which will be published in 2021. At the same time, I am writing the prequel to my paranormal detective series, the first book in the series, '*Welcome To Witherleigh*' which was published last year.

P.J. Reed